Job Seeker's Insider Series

Ignite Your LinkedIn Profile

Learn the Secrets to How LinkedIn Ranking Really Works

Donald J Wittman

ISBN: 978-1-7338059-0-2

I would like to dedicate this book to the following people:

My Parents

They have always wanted me to be successful with all the endeavors I have jumped into. My parents, growing up in the Great Depression, stressed the need to work hard. One of the big things that the Depression taught was that you need to keep friends and family close because they are all you have when things get bad. This passion to help others came into focus when I was doing some consulting and learning how LinkedIn works. They understood that being out of a job was a challenging time and that we need to help each other. My friends from the HERT and SERT Networking groups got me thinking where I came from and that it was time to help others. It finally sank in, and I am feeling more in touch with people than I have ever been. So Mom and Dad, thank you for getting me to where I feel I belong.

My Son, Stephen

Stephen has been a great help with this book. He helped me to focus on talking simpler and explaining more. It is difficult not to speak geek when talking about a subject like LinkedIn. I have spent most of my professional life getting straight to the point. I generally assumed that the people listening to me have enough background to get into the meat of the topic. This is a huge mind-shift for me.

My Wife, Regina

Regina has been very tolerant and supportive of my going solo with my career change. We have had a great time traveling before this change. Her belief that things will get better has been a great lift for me when things looked dim. I cannot thank her enough for her support.

DOWNLOAD

THE AUDIOBOOK **FREE!**

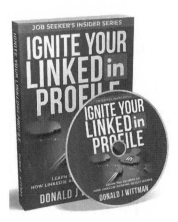

**Just To say Thanks for downloading my Book, I
would like to offer you the Audiobook version
100% FREE!**

WWW.wittmantechnology.com/free-ignite

Contents

Introduction

"Why isn't LinkedIn working for me?"

The simple answer is very few people understand how LinkedIn works. Many of the free courses only address the initial setup of a LinkedIn profile. Even many of the paid courses out there don't do anything beyond the basics.

Many of the courses do not even tell you the basics. Some of the courses spend a lot of time on branding. Others work on making your profile look professional or teaching you how to use generic keywords. These steps are backward; they are the last things you should do not the first things you should do.

The first thing you need to do is to be visible to the recruiter, no one that I have found is covering this. The second thing is to find current and specific keywords for the position you are looking for, not generic position keywords. Without these two, recruiters are not going to find you Via LinkedIn search. After all, why are you on LinkedIn if not to be found by a recruiter or potential client?

One of the best lines I have heard from LinkedIn professionals is that "we are just going to put your resume into your LinkedIn profile. Then we will pretty it up a bit, and you will be good to go!" This line could not be further from the truth!

LinkedIn is a search engine. To make LinkedIn work, you have to feed it the information it wants to get the results you need. To use a good analogy, if you are going to cook a meal for your family, and you have all the ingredients but nothing to cook it with, you will have a problem with it coming out very well, if at all edible. The same thing with LinkedIn. You can have the most beautifully written profile, but if you do not give LinkedIn the food it needs, the search for you will fail. Keywords are the food LinkedIn needs for the position you want, or you will not have the result you want. The result you want is to be found by recruiters. This is the problem most LinkedIn users find themselves in.

When job seekers finally land a job, the most common comment that I have received is "I will always be prepared." The training and consulting I've done in the last seven years is that "I will never, ever be unprepared for a potential jobless event. My LinkedIn profile is always updated religiously."

I have had people prepare their LinkedIn profile for the next potential position right after they have landed a job. This tells me how uncertain the job market is. With all the company buyouts and automation projects, the most stable companies are looking to size their staff for efficiency. An extreme example is one of my clients in the medical device arena. He has looked for a new job every year for the last four years because there are so many mergers and acquisitions in his industry. The other area is the outsourcing craze. Companies are saying, "If the business function is not critical to the success of the business, why are we managing it? Let's outsource it to allow the company to focus on what is most important."

This is the introduction book to my Job Pull Strategy. In this book, you will learn the value of building a searchable LinkedIn profile that ranks is search via both LinkedIn and Google. This book takes you through the basics of what you need to put in place to show up on the first page. It starts out with the assumption that you have already set up a LinkedIn profile for yourself. We will start by going over some LinkedIn background and statistics to better understand why we are doing this. We will then go through a LinkedIn profile checklist, which sets the stage to make everything work. We will then move into what affects LinkedIn visibility. We will cover how to find keywords for the position you want at a high level. Then we will move on to identifying the high-value areas of a LinkedIn profile. We will do a profile search example to understand what we are doing.

I started out helping people with LinkedIn while I was searching for a new job myself. I ended up reverse engineering how LinkedIn search worked. I tested my Keyword Strategy for many months. This Keyword Strategy allows me to put almost any person who is in a job search on page 1 for the position they are seeking. I call this process my Job Pull Strategy System. Others may call it an Inbound Marketing Strategy or Pull Marketing Strategy.

My friends were my first guinea pigs as I developed this system. It was them who pushed me to develop my webinar series and write this book. It is their positive results that gave me the confidence to put together my company. My consulting business helps the job seeker and small business move to the next level. I teach seminars for groups in New York City, Connecticut, and Massachusetts once a year.

When one of these seminars was canceled because of an impending snowstorm, several people emailed and asked whether we were having the seminar or not. They said that they would travel through the snowstorm rather than miss my seminar.

I am a recovering Chief Technology Officer who likes to help people in a positive way. So digging into LinkedIn was a natural curiosity for me. Just like Google, LinkedIn is a search engine. The difference between LinkedIn and Google is that their search algorithms make different assumptions.

Most people who utilize the strategies outlined in this book have more "LinkedIn search appearances." Your "Who viewed your profile" appearances will also increase in your LinkedIn Dashboard. These results are from my 30-minute follow-up calls after many of my webinars. Some professionals have very challenging positions that may need much more detailed help. They attend the more advanced seminar for "More Powerful Search Ranking." Those who took this seminar had significant increases in their dashboard counts. These results are very common for those who apply my strategies. There is no guessing with my seminars or books; it lays it out for you in a simple-to-understand "how to" method.

The strategy helps you walk through what recruiters are looking for when they search for a position they are trying to fill. Recruiters use a very straightforward strategy. Recruiters first search for:

- Job title

- Job attributes

- Keywords

- Company fit

The biggest thing that most people don't address is visibility. We go through what visibility is and how it affects your profile on LinkedIn later in the book. Without visibility on LinkedIn, no matter what you do to get traffic to your profile, it won't work. So there are three things we're going to address in this book. They are:

- Visibility

- Functional fit

- Company fit

These three things will dramatically change how your LinkedIn profile works. We will go over why you are not getting search appearances, and we will see why the search appearances are driving profile views. Current statistics tell us that it takes, on average, 1,000 general page views or 300 recruiter views to get a job offer. With this strategy, we will greatly enhance your ability to be found by a recruiter. This will help your understanding of what you have to do to make ongoing changes to adapt to the current job market. The class that started all this is my most popular seminar/webinar: Tips, Tricks, and Strategy to be Found on LinkedIn. It has helped thousands of people find their next job. I hope you will read this book and join those who have transitioned their career to the next opportunity.

With these strategies, you will find that you are spending more time answering recruiters' contacts than posting on job boards. This seminar/webinar helped job seekers get two to three inbound recruiter contacts a week when properly implemented.

It takes approximately 80 hours to put this strategy in place. There are no shortcuts to this implementation. If you have problems implementing these strategies, you may need the more advanced book. *The Job Seekers Guide to Getting Hired On LinkedIn* goes into more detail on the functional fit areas of this strategy.

It is painful for me to hear people say that they have been in transition for many months and have made little progress in their job search. I met with a friend who had paid for a very expensive job search package. This included a resume, LinkedIn profile, and extra job search collateral. He was making very little progress in the last six months with his job search. He attended my Tips and Tricks webinar class. We had a follow-up coffee meeting, and two weeks later, he was knee deep in interviews. So if you are not having success, this is the place to get moving in your job search.

Chapter 1
LinkedIn Background and Statistics

A job search today can be visualized as a three-legged stool:

The first leg of the stool is a **job push strategy**, which is approximately 10%–20% of the job landings. The job push strategy is the most traditional part of the job search strategy. This is where the job seeker responds to job boards, job advertisements, contingent and retained recruiters. Job seekers will research current open positions, contact and work with recruiters. This part of the job search used to be about 50% of the job search landings. The competitive nature of the contingent recruiting and retained recruiting has become less of the job search market.

The second leg of the stool is the **job networking strategy**, which is approximately 30%–40% of job landings. Networking is a very successful method for landing mid-level to senior positions. There are a couple of sides of a job networking strategy. The first part of a networking strategy is going to networking events to meet people from various industries that can help you with contacts in your target companies. The second part is networking with people at your target company, then using those contacts to find or create an open position at your target company. The third part is using LinkedIn or other social media platforms to make connections with employees of your target company, then using those contacts to find and land a position.

The third leg of the stool is the **job pull strategy**, which is approximately 30%–40% of job landings. The job pull strategy utilizes one of the social networking sites, such as LinkedIn, Facebook, and Google Plus. Today, LinkedIn is the most advanced and highly utilized social networking platform for job searches. There are other specialized social media platforms for job searching, but most of them have not reached the critical masses as LinkedIn has. Social networking sites are listings of people, capabilities, and attributes. Most of the tools that social networking sites have for job seekers are implemented toward the recruiter and not toward the job seeker. The whole idea of this book prepares the job seeker's profile so that it can be found by the recruiters.

Ninety percent of recruiters will not look at your profile if you do not have the following:

- A photo that does not convert to a thumbnail for search results

- 500 first-level connections

- Your contact information in your summary

- Your resume copied straight into your LinkedIn profile

- A profile that is easily readable via mobile and desktop

A Good Photo

A professional photo on LinkedIn is typically a headshot. Most recruiters believe that they can tell a lot about someone's personality just by looking at their picture. It is important to have a professional smile and a likable demeanor in your photo. Below you'll find a silly example of what not to do.

Attributes of a Good Photo:

a. You do not necessarily need to use a professional photographer as long as you have a good camera or high-quality cell phone to take the picture.

b. The camera should be above eye level of the picture candidate to reduce the elongation of the neck and face.

c. The subject should be dressed in the appropriate business attire for the position they are pursuing.

d. The picture background should be white or some other light neutral color.

e. The light for the picture should be coming from behind the photographer. This will allow the subject's face to be well lit.

f. The picture of the candidate should be from the shoulders to the top of the head. The subject does not necessarily have to be in the exact center of the picture. It can be off to the side or slightly high, but it should be close to the center.

g. A high percentage of recruiters believe they can gain insights about the pictured candidate's personality. They try to read the facial expression of the subject. It is important that you have a professional smile and a pleasant demeanor in your picture. This will give a good personal impression to the recruiter. There are online picture-review sites that can help you.

h. Many people say that natural light is better than artificial light when taking someone's photo. However, getting the right amount of natural light coming from the right direction is not always that simple. Good artificial light from a set of "daylight" light bulbs can be as good as natural light.

i. Do not try to take a "funny face" picture.

j. It should be noted that "LinkedIn Photo Guidelines" reserve the right to remove your photo if it is not a likeness of you or a headshot photo. If you put a photo of a company logo, landscape, animal, word, or phrase in the photo area, LinkedIn can remove it without notice.

k. Minimum dot pitch for a LinkedIn photo is 400 X 400 pixels. The maximum is 20,000 X 20,000 pixels. The photo must be in a PNG, JPG, or a GIF format. I tell most people to use 400 X 400 pixels.

LinkedIn has a blog post on their official LinkedIn blog with more photo information.

"The LinkedIn Guide to the Perfect #WorkSelfie"

--- or--

https://blog.linkedin.com/2015/04/29/linkedin-guide-to-the-perfect-workselfie?trk=li__namer_bcs_always on18_blog_profile_photo&utm_campaign=alwayson18 &utm_medium=blog&utm_source=blog&utm_content =profile_photo

Two Good Profile Photos:

Six Poor Profile Photos:

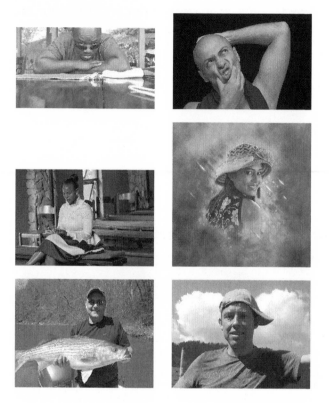

So let's talk about your thumbnail photo that shows up in a LinkedIn search, which is the first thing recruiters see when you show up in a search. Most recruiters will not choose your profile if your thumbnail photo is not showing up. There are two reasons this will happen. First, the photo is the wrong size or pitch. Second, LinkedIn is having trouble rendering it as a thumbnail or you do not have a photo at all. Make sure your photo works properly. It is very easy to test. All you have to do is a LinkedIn search that you know your profile should show up in and see if your thumbnail photo appears properly. If it's not, or it takes more than a few seconds to render, that means something is wrong. Please fix it quickly so that you are not passed over in searches in the future.

LinkedIn Search Thumbnail:

Nancy Nelson • 1st
CIO, COO
Greater New York City Area

Current: Resource Management Executive,

377 shared connections

Check out the *Official LinkedIn Blog* for "The LinkedIn Guide to the Perfect #WorkSelfie"

-- or--

https://blog.linkedin.com/2015/04/29/linkedin-guide-to-the-perfect-workselfie?trk=li__namer_bcs_always on18_blog_profile_photo&utm_campaign=alwayson18 &utm_medium=blog&utm_source=blog&utm_content =profile_photo

500 First-Level Connections

LinkedIn no longer penalizes you if you do not have 500 first-level connections. They now only require 50 first-level connections to have a complete or all-star profile. Recruiters believe that if you don't have 500 first-level connections, you're not serious about your LinkedIn profile. Recruiters understand that not having 500 first-level connections will reduce your appearance in LinkedIn searches. As such, they believe they can immediately eliminate you as a potential job candidate.

Ranking high on a LinkedIn search has become much more competitive. Having 500 first-level connections worked well five years ago. Today, you need between 5,000 and 8,000 first-level connections to have the same level of success. The reduction in the number of first-level connections is the foundation of how LinkedIn makes money. The last set of statistics tells that more than 50% of LinkedIn revenue comes from the HR or Enterprise subscriptions. The recruiters need you to have many connections. This keeps them from having very expensive HR or Enterprise LinkedIn subscriptions, which start at $900 per month.

Do Not Paste Your Resume Into LinkedIn

Many LinkedIn members will cut and paste their resume into their LinkedIn profiles. Most recruiters want to see more about you and about what you do. A cold resume gives the recruiters only the most basic details of your previous work history. LinkedIn is a social networking site, and recruiters expect you to talk more about yourself as it relates to your position. They do not want just the group of cold descriptors that are on your resume.

Resumes are typically searched via the Application Tracking Systems. They use a search system much like

Microsoft Word. It only takes a single search hit occurrence to have a positive outcome with the search algorithm. This will get you on the review hit list.

LinkedIn's search algorithm more closely emulates Google rather than Application Tracking System. The LinkedIn search algorithm is a points-based system. It cares how many points you get on a given search. This is a very different philosophy compared to an Application Tracking System.

94% Of Recruiters Use LinkedIn To Vet Candidates' Resumes

When a recruiter looks at your resume, you should have an active link to LinkedIn. They will undoubtedly compare what your resume says with what your LinkedIn profile says. It is important not to contradict your resume with your LinkedIn profile content.

LinkedIn should be a superset of your resume(s). If you're writing a specific resume for a specific job opportunity, it cannot contradict what is in your LinkedIn profile. A recruiter wants to gain extra insights from your LinkedIn profile as compared to what they read on your resume. The more insights you can provide a recruiter via your profile, the more comfortable they will feel submitting you to a hiring manager. Recruiters believe candidates with positive details in their LinkedIn profiles are more qualified than those with just resumes.

Listing Skills Increases Profile Page Views By Thirteen Times

Listing your skills on LinkedIn is a little tricky. I tell my clients to use their keywords in the "Skills" section. You have to make sure that the skills you are using are keywords from the "Skills" pulldown box. If they are not in the pulldown box, you will not get search points for them.

Skills are separately searchable items which are part of what the sales navigator and Enterprise/HR search for. So if you don't have your keywords in the LinkedIn Skills search area, a recruiter can miss them if they are specifically looking for them in the Skills area. Many people claim that having others endorse your skills is a very meaningless endeavor. Recruiters still take them into account if you have a significant number of endorsements. It's really up to you to find and use this section; it can be a huge help for most people who are in the job search. I tell people that everyone in the group should be endorsing each member for all their skills— allowing them to get enough endorsements to be meaningful for the recruiter.

Unless you have 25 endorsements for each skill, it's just not fruitful to a recruiter. So reach out to your friends and get your skills endorsed. It shouldn't take you all that long—just a little bit of emailing and some dedication. Most people are more than willing to endorse your skills. There is more of an upside to getting endorsements than there is a downside, so I suggest you spend a little time to get this done. They will stay with you forever, so you merely have to do it once.

Many Firms Have Outsourced First And Second Level Research

Many firms have outsourced their first- and second-level job-search research outside the US. These recruiters, for the most part, use LinkedIn as their sole pool of candidates for the position that they are researching. Most of these outsourced firms cannot use candidates' resumes. Most resumes have too much PII data (Personally Identifiable Information) in them. Most recruiting organizations do not believe it is a good idea to have this information outside the United States. Outsourced firms do not want to take on the responsibility for shipping resumes outside the United States and getting sued for having PII data released. So not only do they not send them resumes, most of these researchers only utilize the basic LinkedIn subscription. This causes problems with their ability to see the entire LinkedIn membership. As a result, many LinkedIn subscribers put a word-based resume as an attachment to their LinkedIn profile with much of the PII data removed. This subject is discussed in more detail in later books.

One In Twenty LinkedIn Members Are Recruiters

Because one in 20 LinkedIn members are recruiters, this gives most job seekers a large pool of potential connections they can make. Recruiters connect with recruiters, thereby giving you more visibility to other recruiters. Since most recruiters do not have the HR or Enterprise LinkedIn subscriptions, having lots of first-level connections makes searching easier. One of the big things I tell job seekers is that recruiters are their buddies. Connect with recruiters who recruit in your field of endeavor. Since recruiters are the most likely to connect with you, it gives you a large pool of folks to become first-level connections with. You can never have enough first-level connections.

How to search for recruiters to connect with is covered in the other books in this series titled, *Advanced Search* and *Is Your LinkedIn Strategy Failing?*

Seven Out Of Ten 18- to 35-year-old Professionals Find Their Jobs Via Social Media

Two years ago, this number was less than five out of ten who used social media as their primary source for their job search. It is expected that this evolution will continue and expand upward of 35-year-olds. You are beginning to see more senior job seekers getting their first contact from a LinkedIn source.

The traditional job search is changing in the market to allow for expediency. One of the reasons social media is working and is being accepted more and more often is that the traditional mechanism has become very costly. Many job descriptions for positions have been dumbed down for legal purposes. This allows companies more flexibility in their hiring. This means that they have to address more and more job applications before they find a suitable candidate.

Many companies who are recruiting above the most junior people are seeing only one good resume out of every 300 to 400 submissions. If you look at the math of what it costs to go through this many applicants, you'll find the number is staggering. If the HR manager is going to submit 20 job applicants to the hiring manager, that would mean that they have to go through at least 6,000 job applications.

If you do the math, it's 6,000 times five minutes to process each applicant via the Application Tracking System, which gives you 30,000 minutes. Then 30,000 minutes divided by 60 minutes per hour gives you 500 hours. This breaks down to 12 to 13 weeks, depending on your workweek. This is why LinkedIn is becoming more popular every year.

Chapter 2
Functional Fit

Overview of Functional Fit

We raised the topic of Functional Fit in the Introduction. Functional Fit is important because it comes from the job requirements listed in the job description for the hiring position. A recruiter will break down the requirements from the high points, which will then be used as keywords. Usually, a single job requirement is a short sentence.

Keywords are the next level of specificity, which are generally one to five words long. Technology positions have one- to three-word keyword strings. Marketing positions have two- to five-word keyword strings. Some outlier positions have keyword/keyword strings up to seven words long. The recruiters use these keywords to search for prospective job candidates.

Kforce is a nationwide recruiting firm that surveyed many recruiters. They first wanted to find out the size of the keyword search strings recruiters are using. Next, they wanted to find the content of LinkedIn search strings recruiters are using. All this to find prospective job candidates more reliably. Their results are below.

Kforce Keyword Statistics – search keywords:

- Minimum five keywords/keyword strings plus title

- Maximum 16 keywords/keyword strings plus title

- Average 12 keywords/keyword strings plus title

I have tested over a thousand clients' LinkedIn profiles. The job seeker's target "position title" testing has resulted in 80% not having their target "position title" rank in LinkedIn search on the first three pages in their target market.

Why is it important to rank in the first three pages? Look below at another Kforce survey. If the recruiter search does not show up on the first three pages (or the first 22 profile results) the average recruiter will not find you.

Kforce Statistics search profile visited:

- Minimum eight profiles visited

- Maximum 50 profiles visited

- Average 22 profiles visited

The testing I have conducted for "Position Keywords" is as problematic with job seekers as position title results. I asked the same clients for their top ten target "Position Keywords" so I could test them. Approximately 50% did not know or have ten "Position Keywords/Keyword

Strings" identified. Of those that did have their target position keywords identified: less than 80% had more than four "Position Keywords" ranked on the first three pages in their target local job market, less than 20% had five to six keywords ranked on the first three pages in their target market, and less than one percent had all ten ranked on the first three pages in their target local job market. The statistics above demonstrate that if you do not show up on the first three pages, you are unlikely to show up in the average search by a recruiter.

What does all this mean? I try to get my clients to identify 20 keywords/keyword strings to help develop their search testing that will rank in searches.

In Chapter 4 we will do an overview of a process to find position keywords.

Recruiters will only visit enough LinkedIn profiles to meet the requirements of the position search. So let's say they have to find twenty potential job candidates that meet the provided job requirements. This is, by the way, more than normal.

Let's assume that the search yields an 80% success rate; then the recruiter will not go past page three (or 24 profiles). If we go so far as to say that there is only a 50% success rate, that is still only four LinkedIn search pages. So what does this mean, if you are not on the first three pages of a position search? That means you are not going to be found by the recruiter or researcher. How to test your LinkedIn search position and keywords is in the book *The Job Seekers Guide to Getting Hired On LinkedIn.*

LinkedIn Versus ATS Search

An ATS system (Applicant Tracking System) manages resumes and job applications. This application uses a Microsoft Word-like search functionality with partial fit results that provides maximum user inclusion. The ATS system typically uses a non-points-based result. Search results for the ATS system can be adjusted using various parameters to give more meaningful results. This is sometimes a hindrance and sometimes a blessing. Sometimes it is called fuzzy logic results.

LinkedIn provides exact-fit point-based probabilistic search results. LinkedIn search results offer a Boolean search capability that cannot be adjusted for fuzzy logic results. LinkedIn only understands exact matches. LinkedIn has dabbled with title adaption, such as VP for Vice President, but the results have been inconsistent.

Chapter 3
LinkedIn Profile Checklist

Your LinkedIn Profile Must Be 100% Complete

If your profile is not 100% complete, you will see a box that looks like the one below. This Profile Strength box tells you the strength which LinkedIn has broken down into five levels:

1. Beginner

2. Intermediate

3. Advanced

4. Expert

5. All-Star

Profile Strength: **Intermediate**

Which university or school did you attend?
Add your school so that classmates and alumni can easily find you

If you click on the next button shown above, LinkedIn with walk you through what is missing. This feature has been brought back and is very helpful to most beginners and those trying to use the help files, which tend to be confusing.

What do you need to get to an "All-Star" profile strength?

Your LinkedIn profile needs to be 100% complete to rank best in a search. This means you should have an All-Star LinkedIn profile. Your profile strength shows up on your LinkedIn Dashboard in the upper right-hand side as shown below.

I am not going to cover what you need for each level of profile strength. Instead, I am just going to cover the "All-Star" profile level of strength.

A. Profile picture

B. Industry

C. Location

D. Summary (three full lines, some say 200 to 500 characters)

E. Experience (current position plus two previous positions)

F. Skills (five skills or more)

G. Education

H. Connections (need at least 50 connections)

You Are No Longer Required To Have Recommendations

You need to be careful with recommendations because they are considered part of the search text of your LinkedIn profile. If you have too many recommendations or the recommendations are long, this can impact search results. The amount of additional text of the recommendations can work against you in LinkedIn searches. LinkedIn search works on keyword density; the more text you have, the more keywords you need to rank. We will talk more about what makes up this problem later in the book.

Use LinkedIn Locations

You should use LinkedIn locations rather than the city you live in, which is the first graphic below. LinkedIn has broken the mapping between the city and LinkedIn locations almost every year. When LinkedIn makes updates to their LinkedIn search algorithm, LinkedIn locations generally break. If your "city" and the mapping of "city" to "LinkedIn Locations" is broken, you will not show up in recruiter searches. Most recruiters use LinkedIn locations in their job candidate searches, which is shown in the second graphic below.

Country/Region *	ZIP code
United States ▾	06877

Locations within this area

Ridgefield, Connecticut ▾

Country/Region *	ZIP code
United States ▾	06877

Locations within this area

Greater New York City Area ▾

I had quite a few clients not get found in search for up to two months when LinkedIn locations mapping was having difficulties. You can see the use of LinkedIn locations (Greater New York City Area) below with Nancy's profile.

Nancy Nelson • 1st

CIO, COO

Greater New York City Area

Current: Resource Management Executive,

377 shared connections

Your Default LinkedIn Headline

Your LinkedIn headline is the first thing that recruiters are going to see when they choose to view your profile. LinkedIn defaults to a merging of your title and company from your current position in your experience area. Titles are the wrong thing to have in your main headline. When someone searches for your current position, they are searching the headline of your current position, not your main headline of your LinkedIn profile. Recruiters will know if you do not customize your main headline.

Your LinkedIn Profile Needs A Great Headline

Your main headline should tell the recruiter what your "High Value" skills are, what are you an expert at, and what made you succeed.

You can write a great headline in two different ways or a combination of both. The first and simplest is using individual keywords, keyword pairs, or keyword triplets separated by vertical bars. The second is by a complex sentence or a combination of both. For those who have a good marketing knack, the complex sentence is what I prefer. A few examples are below:

Strategy | Transformation | Sales | Direct Marketing | Change Management | Business Development | Strategic Marketing

Blockchain Expert | Digital Marketing and Branding Expert | ICO Marketing | Social Media Strategist

Safety Personnel | Administrative Support | Client Relations | Project Manager | Customer Service

Award-Winning Design Leader Who Engineers and Implements Next Generation Solutions and Results-Driven Initiatives

Branding is important in the selection of your keywords you use in your headlines. You also use keywords in other high-value areas of your LinkedIn profile. If you do not put your main headline keywords in your other headlines, they may not be searchable. I only suggest using your title in your main headline if your search results for your title is not ranking in search. The main headline of your LinkedIn profile is the most important part of your profile. The next most important is your current position and your most current three previous positions of your LinkedIn profile. Take great care to utilize them for your important keywords and job attributes.

A Powerful LinkedIn Summary

Your LinkedIn summary is your marketing pitch. Please make sure your summary does not read like a resume. You want it to be personable, you want to use friendly language, and you want to show a little bit about yourself. Most recruiters hate it when people put resume speak in their LinkedIn summary. Your summary should answer the question: Why should I hire you?

Your LinkedIn summary is the most powerful part of your LinkedIn profile from a recruiter's point of view. It tells the recruiter what you have done and what you can do for them. Put in your summary an opening statement about who you are and what makes you successful. The first three lines in your summary are the best real estate of your summary. It shows up when someone looks at your main LinkedIn profile page. You should make these three lines count as an invitation for them to read further.

I recommend that you include three examples of your major successes. You should tell your story—such as what made you successful and what successes you had. For example:

HIGHLY AVAILABLE SYSTEMS

One of companies biggest challenges was to address the uptime availability of the company's website. By using a group of five highly available systems enhancements, we were able to get our production websites to 99.99% availability.

This project brought the company the equivalent of 13 extra business days of demand generation the next year.

Have Your Contact Information In Your Summary

At the end of your summary, you should put a CTA (call to action) in the closing statement to get them to contact you about a potential position. This should be followed immediately by your contact information. See below my call to action:

CONTACT ME

I'd welcome the opportunity to schedule a time to talk about your LinkedIn challenges and explore how we may be able to work together. I teach seminars, workshops and provide one-on-one tutoring and coaching to clients looking to strengthen their presence on LinkedIn.

I can be reached at:
email-don@don.com
Telephone-333-444-555

One of the big problems we discuss later is that only about a third of recruiters have the Enterprise or HR LinkedIn subscription. This allows them to see everyone on LinkedIn along with their contact information. So for the remaining recruiters who do not have these expensive subscriptions and are not a first-level to you, you have to have your contact information in your summary.

Your LinkedIn Profile Must Be In Sync With Your Resume

You must maintain your LinkedIn profile such that it is in sync with the resumes that you send out. As I mentioned before, 90+% of recruiters will validate your resume against your LinkedIn profile. It is a necessity to make sure that your resume does not contradict your LinkedIn profile. Most recruiters will reject an applicant if this is the case.

Have Statistics Tell Your Story

You should have statistics about your successes in your current experience position and previous experience positions in your profile to support your summary statements. Even if the company you work for does not allow you to use the statistics directly, it is possible to obfuscate them enough so that they are not company confidential information. Recruiters are looking for statistics in your profile to amplify your successes and what they can potentially expect of you in the future, so please don't overlook this item.

Some examples:

- Dollars saved

- Dollar sales increase

- Percent better

- Percent increase

- Percent productivity increase

- Productivity improvement

- Time-to-market improvement

- Workforce savings

- Supply chain improvements

- Tax savings

- Agility improvements

- Capital savings

- Expense reduction

Extension To Your Name Line

LinkedIn is now allowing you to put certifications and degrees at the end of your name line. To be clear, LinkedIn still says in your user agreement that you should not use it for anything but your name. However, LinkedIn has not been enforcing this rule. This area is a high-point area of LinkedIn, so it is a very valuable area to put your keywords.

It is important that you still maintain your first name and initials in the first box and your last name at the beginning of the second box. After your name, you can put degrees or certifications, but be careful not to put in too much. Sometimes this will cause your name to no longer be searchable. You should not put your first and last name in the first name box and fill your last name box with titles and certifications. There is a high probability that a recruiter or anyone will not be able to find your profile by a name search in the standard search box. If the person doing the searching has a paid LinkedIn subscription, they have more ways to search, which makes this less of an issue. Approximately 50% do not have a paid subscription, so it's best to not overuse these fields. You can see examples below.

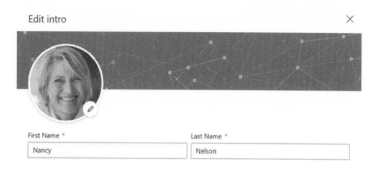

Standard Name Field Usage

Standard Name Field Usage With Certifications And Degrees

Edit intro ✕

First Name *

Nancy Nelson

Last Name *

CIO, COO, MBA, CISSP, CMA (123)-555-9876

Do Not Do This With The Standard Name Field

Chapter 4
Punctuation, Readability, And Fonts

Your LinkedIn Profile Must Be Easy To Read

Your LinkedIn profile's readability is very important to the first and second level of recruiters. There are two factors in readability. So this means the first factor is white space, so the text is not just a big blob. The average first- and second-level recruiters are sometimes called *researchers*. They typically only have to read your summary and experience headlines. If there is not enough white space in your summary to break up the text, it is very difficult to read physically. The second factor is sentence complexity. It is considered best to write your profile at an eighth-grade level or lower. If you don't have a tool to do this, keeping sentences smaller than 18 words will help.

The typical first- and second-level recruiters have small screens on their computers. LinkedIn has changed the font color from black to gray, which makes it more difficult to stand out on a small screen. LinkedIn claims it is easier on the eyes. Some research reinforces this, but my experience (and complaints from others) contradicts this.

If you're someone (like a recruiter) who is reading resumes and LinkedIn profiles a large part of their day, gray is more taxing on their eyes than black. So be kind to the first and second level of recruiters and make it more readable. We will talk about some examples of this later on.

The other problem with your profile not being easy to read is when it is read on a mobile phone, it may look like a blob of text on a phone screen. So be aware of this, and we will see some examples later on what to do to make it a little more readable.

Your Profile Must Have Plenty Of White Space

Your LinkedIn profile must be easy to read. You should not have more than seven lines without a line break. I prefer to make most paragraphs in my summary no more than three or four lines. It is sometimes impossible to do this. A seven-line paragraph in your summary on a normal PC ends up being a 20-line blob of text on your mobile phone. 60+% of all profile views on LinkedIn are viewed on a mobile device. If you don't make it easy to view on a desktop, it will be horrible on a mobile device. See the examples below.

Example Of A Good Summary Via Desktop:

If your LINKEDIN PROFILE was on PAGE 1 for your JOB SEARCH or BUSINESS, what kind of success would that bring to the table? LinkedIn is the best place for business people to find other business people.

As a previous CTO, I combine in-depth technology expertise toward the use of LinkedIn. I have a set of processes to get my clients found. For those DIY'ers, I offer a variety of Training Classes and Webinars to help you understand my proven process.

HIGH CHALLENGE JOB SEARCH

The most common complaint, after professionals complete their LinkedIn Profiles, is Head Hunters are not finding them on LinkedIn.

I help Professionals find the right "KEYWORDS" for the position they aspire to and place these words in my client's profile for the best search results.

This is only one of five metrics that are important to LinkedIn Search. This process results in significantly

Example Of A Good Summary On A Mobile Phone:

Be More Visible on LinkedIn With a Search Optimized Profile | LinkedIn Consultant | LinkedIn Training | LinkedIn Author

If your LINKEDIN PROFILE was on PAGE 1 for your JOB SEARCH or BUSINESS, what kind of success would that bring to the table? LinkedIn is the best places for business people to find other business people.

As a previous CTO, I combine in-depth technology expertise toward the use of LinkedIn. I have a set of processes to get my clients found. For those DIY'ers, I offer a variety of Training Classes and Webinars to help you understand my proven process.

HIGH CHALLENGE JOB SEARCH

The most common complaint, after professionals complete their LinkedIn Profiles, is Head Hunters are not finding them on LinkedIn.

I help Professionals find the right "KEYWORDS" for the position they aspire to and place these words in my client's profile for the best search results.

Example Of A Bad Summary On A Desktop:

How do you choose a franchise with 4000+ brands in the market today? I consult with corporate professionals and new entrepreneurs to determine if business ownership is the best next chapter for you! Work feels quite different when your talent and time is invested in a business that's your own. As a multi-brand franchise owner myself, I am uniquely qualified to guide you through a process designed to sort through the clutter, dispel the myths and uncover the meaningful data points in choosing the best franchise for you while minimizing your risk.
> > Understand You First
Before pinpointing the best franchises opportunities that fulfill your lifestyle and financial goals, career aspirations and leverage your skills and talents, I get to know you first.
> > Develop Your Strategy
We take it all into consideration - your preferred geography, your family situation, your desired role in the
business, your comfort level for financing and your timeline.
> > Identify the Best Opportunities

Example Of A Bad Summary On A Mobile Phone:

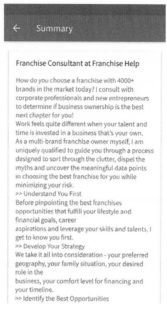

Limit Boolean Operators, Punctuation, And Custom Fonts

There are two main reasons to limit Boolean operators in your LinkedIn profile. The first we talked about earlier, some of LinkedIn Boolean operators are also punctuation. LinkedIn has issues with parsing punctuation properly. LinkedIn has some issues in search of punctuation other than the use of periods and commas.

If you have a keyword phrase such as "network technology:" in many cases, the search for "network technology" will fail. Because after technology, the ":" has become part of the word "technology." This is true of much of the standard punctuation we use. There is no documentation on this anywhere that I can find. When doing testing on clients' profiles, this is the case most of the time. I should say that this is not always the case, but it happens often enough to take note of. I take precautions to leave a space on both sides of most punctuation. There are some exceptions, such as "M&A" and "P&L," which work correctly.

I recommend my clients use spaces between most punctuation other than periods and commas. It is a lot of work to test keywords in your LinkedIn profile. It is easier to assume this is always the case rather than spending hours validating if keywords are properly resolving in a LinkedIn search.

To be a real buster, I believe LinkedIn should put the search feature back into their product, which highlighted the words that were identified/found in a search. It used to be that keyword search results with more than five search elements would come back highlighted when you looked in a LinkedIn search. This was one of the best tools to help figure out why your LinkedIn profile was not ranking properly. It was also true that this did not work in every browser, but it helped job seekers understand their profile ranking better.

The second reason it is a good idea to limit Boolean operators in your LinkedIn profile for both Google and LinkedIn is that it is not unusual for both search engines to get confused with embedded Boolean operators in the

LinkedIn profile text. I will agree the problem is not consistent, but it happens often enough to take care when using them. The Google Boolean operators are: &, /,-,(,). And LinkedIn Boolean operators are:-, (,), NOT, OR, AND. LinkedIn does not officially tell you to limit these; however, in advanced searches, they sometimes cause problems. This is especially true when you're doing complex advance searches. I have had difficulties with having Boolean operators in the body of the profile.

Use Of Custom Fonts

LinkedIn now allows you to apply to job postings with your LinkedIn profile and attached resume. Many profiles use fancy bullets in the text of the "Summary and Experience" area. They may also add fancy lightning bolts with or without color. This is not a good idea since most Application Tracking Systems that interface with LinkedIn do not like non-standard fonts. If you want to submit a job application via your LinkedIn profile, you should stick to standard fonts like Times New Roman, Arial, and Calibri. Why am even talking about this? Many times, Application Tracking Systems do not support complex fonts. So what happens to your rejected application submission? Rejected job applications go to the ATS manual queue. Most companies do not try to recover rejected job application submissions, so they end up in the bit bucket.

Some examples of arrows, pointers, and symbols to stay away from:

Having your resume on LinkedIn is a great way to help recruiters and can be used for job submission as well. LinkedIn did not support Microsoft "doc" or "docx" formats a couple of years ago. So many LinkedIn members started to use PDF formatted resumes. PDF resumes are problematic because only a small number of Application Tracking Systems support PDF documents. Some PDF converters use features not generically supported. The result is many times these PDF resumes end up in the bit bucket as well. When I was looking for a job, I was constantly reminded by recruiters and headhunters that I needed to submit my resume in a Word document format.

Below is an example of resume competencies:

These competencies should also be in your LinkedIn profile in this form or another. If you list something in your resume, you need to list it in your LinkedIn profile.

Technology and Business Acumen that Optimize Business Results:

- *eCommerce*

- *Automated Quality Process*

- *IT Infrastructure / Telecom / Mobility*

- *Enterprise Turnarounds*

- *Enterprise Security and Compliance*

- *Business Growth Software Development*

- *Datacenter Optimization*

- *Profitability Enhancements*

- *Post-Acquisition System Managers*

- *Governance / Process Improvement*

- *Vendor Sourcing and Negotiations*

- *Team Leadership and Developments*

Below is an example of a resume overview:

These overview items should also be in your LinkedIn profile in this form or another. If you have it in your resume, you need to have it in your LinkedIn profile.

Global, results-driven IT Executive whose technological expertise and business acumen deliver accelerated enterprise-wide solutions on time and under budget. Optimizes results through organization, elimination of bureaucracy, innovation, and collaboration. Builds high-performing teams and develops them to deliver technically superior products and solutions with exceptional customer value. Sought after as knowledge leader on business continuance and security. Navigates with expertise through key life cycle inflection points including critical mergers and acquisitions, organic growth, liquidity events, and turnarounds. Solving the previously unsolvable.

Change Your Default Public URL

Most people consider it poor style to use the automatically generated LinkedIn personal URL. You should change your default public URL to a personalized URL. My public URL is http://www. linkedin.com/in/donaldjwittman. Not changing your default LinkedIn public URL leads people to believe that you are not familiar with the Internet. It demonstrates a lack of knowledge of technology. There are two places to change your public URL. The first place is on your profile page. The second is in your settings. Below are screenshots of each.

Screenshot Of Your Profile Page

Account	Privacy	Ads

How others see your profile and network information

How others see your LinkedIn activity

How LinkedIn uses your data

Job seeking preferences

Blocking and hiding

How others see your profile and network

Edit your public profile

Choose how your profile appears to non-logged in members via search engines or permitted services

Who can see your email address

Choose who can see your email address on your profile

Who can see your connections

Screenshot Of First Settings Page

Public profile settings

You control your profile and can limit what is shown on search engines and other off-LinkedIn services. Viewers who aren't signed in to LinkedIn will see all or some portions of the profile view displayed below.

Nancy Nelson   500+
connections
CIO, COO
Greater New York City Area | Financial Services

Current   Next Generation Marketing Systems, , Chemical Corporation

Previous   Manufacturing Technology, INC. (MTI), Membership Marketing, Beverages USA

🔗 **Edit URL**
Personalize the URL for your profile.

www.linkedin.com/in/nancy-nelson 🖉

Edit Content
This is your public profile. To edit its section update your profile.

Edit contents

👁 **Edit Visibility**
You control your profile's appearance for viewers who are not logged-in members. Limits you set here affect how your profile appears on search engines, profile badges,

Screenshot Of Edit Public Profile Page

Chapter 5
What Affects LinkedIn Search Results

Your LinkedIn profile is ranked by:

- Keywords

- User activity

- User connections

- The number of endorsements you give

- The number of profile page views

- The number of postings

- The number of groups

- The number of endorsements you receive

User activity can help drive profile pages:

- Number of endorsements you give

- Number of level one connections you made

- Number of postings you made

- Number of groups you joined

- The number of recommendations you give

The Number One Thing In Search Is Keywords (Functional Fit)

Let's assume the person who is searching for a great job candidate can see your LinkedIn profile. The next most important thing to your ranking is your keywords. There are two ways keywords are used in LinkedIn searches. The first is keyword density, and the second is keyword frequency. I know this seems pretty foolish, but the LinkedIn profile search is a points-based system. So the longer your LinkedIn profile is, the more frequently you have to put your keywords in your LinkedIn profile to rank in the search. That is why we also talk about keyword density.

Keyword density is the relationship of the amount of text in your profile, including recommendations, to the number of keywords in these areas, titles of your media, titles of attachments, projects, and other areas of your profile. So if you have a 10,000-word LinkedIn profile and you get 100 points in your search words, you have a relationship of one to 100. If you have a 5,000-word LinkedIn profile and you have 100 points, your search words have a relationship of one to 50. The better this relationship, the higher you will rank.

There are two methods to get your keywords to rank:

- Minimalist profile method

- Points-based profile method

The minimalist LinkedIn profile method is relatively simple. It works best for subject matter experts, consultants, and independent professionals. Start out your profile in the same way. You have your professional picture, your name line, your main headline, and your summary. The summary is very focused—start with normal stuff; the first couple lines are what makes you stand out. Then major things like keywords. It's typically half the length of a typical summary (which is normally 2,000 characters).

The big change is in your current position and the next three positions—they need to be filled out, along with your company name. Typically, there are no recommendations to detract from the keyword density. You still have your skills and limited education information. The idea of taking these steps is to get an "All-Star" profile ranking from LinkedIn while leaving out as much low information text as possible.

A points-based LinkedIn profile typically has a well-populated summary and at least four positions in the profile. There is much more detail in the experience areas than in a minimalist profile. Most of these profiles include some recommendations, complete education, and other optional areas, which tends to make profiles long and use a large number of words. The more words in the profile you have, the more you have to repeat the occurrence of keywords for your position to rank well in searches.

The Next Big Thing That Helps Your Rank Is Page Views

If you compare the same profile under two different names, different emails, and different company names (while everything else remains the same):

The first candidate has:

- 8,000 LinkedIn first-level connections

- Ranking in the top 3% viewed within his connections

- 900 page views per 90 days

The second candidate has:

- 2,700 first-level connections

- Ranking in the top 14% viewed within his connections

- 400 pages views per 90 days

So what do you think the difference in search ranking for position title with five keywords in the US for all connection levels is? Not what you would expect.

The first candidate was on page one—Yea!

The second candidate was on page 45, basically lost in the dark depths of LinkedIn—Boo Hoo!

What Are Recruiters Looking For?

- A recruiter will first build a "keywords requirements" list and a potential "nice to have" requirements list.

- Having many first-level and group connections makes your LinkedIn profile more likely to be found by a keyword search.

- LinkedIn is a social media site, so recruiters expect your profile to be more social and have insights about who you are.

Keywords Drive Page Views

- How many profile page views per 90 days do you get?

- It is commonly quoted that you need 1,000 profile page views for your first offer on LinkedIn.

At five profile page views per week, it takes 200 weeks to get 1,000 profile page views.

At ten profile page views per week, it takes 100 weeks to get 1,000 profile page views.

At 25 profile page views per week, it takes 40 weeks to get 1,000 profile page views.

At 50 profile page views per week, it takes 20 weeks to get 1,000 profile page views.

At 100 profile page views per week, it takes ten weeks to get 1,000 profile page views.

Chapter 6
Find Your Keywords

A good friend in a high-level HR role and his team could not find a viable candidate for a critical position for more than two years. He asked for my help finding potential candidates because the senior executives were getting upset (I am being kind here). that their projects were not progressing as originally planned.

I sat down with my friend and his departmental recruiter and went over the job requirements and the formal job description document. The first problem was the published job requirements read as if the position was for an IT person, not a marketing person. The agile requirements were not clear, and their experience level was not evident.

In about two hours, we had a good set of job requirements. Within an hour, I presented them a list of 25 potential candidates within a 25-mile radius (and in their industry). The takeaway is that job requirements need to be clear in the job description to successfully recruit top candidates. That is why I stress that you need to find good and clearly written job descriptions with real job requirements.

Finding Keywords For Your LinkedIn Profile

Finding keywords is a pretty straightforward mechanical process. Depending on your career level, you want five to 20 job descriptions that fit your job goal and fit your experience. A junior-level programmer, marketer, financial, or HR professional should use five to ten job descriptions. A mid-level professional to director-level programmer, marketer, financial, or HR professional should use ten to 15 job descriptions. Senior-level professionals should use 15 to 20 job descriptions.

It is extremely important to find job descriptions for a position that you're looking for and make sure that you have the capabilities to execute the duties for the position properly. You should also take into account which industry you are considering as well. Keywords may differ by industry and may not work well across the board.

The more specific you can be with finding a perfect fit for job descriptions, the better it will work. Recruiters do not want someone who says they can do everything regardless of the industry. Recruiters have a position description, and industry fit, and many of the job requirements can be industry specific. One of the better places to find job descriptions is www.indeed.com.

You need to make sure that the job descriptions you choose have job requirements in them. One of the things I would do is stay away from job descriptions similar to what McKinsey puts out. The McKenzie job descriptions are generally five pages long and have minimal requirement information in them. Many of the job descriptions read like a lot of hot air, but to be fair, many companies are starting to follow this style. Three years ago, 90% of the job descriptions were well written with many primary and secondary job requirements; now it seems to have moved down to 70%.

Recruiters are ditching poor job descriptions and using their own internally developed job requirement lists for the positions they are doing searches for. They are doing their individual research due to the ongoing obfuscation of the real job requirements along with the client-provided job description and job requirements documents. The non-specific job descriptions give hiring managers more flexibility in hiring candidates.

Once you find the job descriptions that fit your ideal job, you cut and paste them into a single Word document. Then you edit out all the company profile information, education requirements, and things that you can control; HR disclaimers, legal disclaimers. Leave only the job requirements. There are two types; the ones that are absolutely required for the position, and those that are nice to have. It is important that you use both sets of job requirements in your keyword discovery process.

Once you remove all of the non-job-requirement information from your Word document, you then cut and paste the document into a word cloud such as www.wordle.net. Most of the word cloud products require JAVA. Make sure your browser can handle JAVA or find one that does not require it. There are many word cloud programs—it may take some time to search or find one, but they are out there.

Wordle.net—landing page

If you click on the "Create" button, you get the page below.

This is the Wordle.net input page. Copy your edited job description document and paste it into the box.

Paste in a bunch of text:

```
1. relationship management and communication skills (written, oral,
interpersonal, presentation, etc)
2. leading projects and managing workload for simultaneous projects.
3. A team player with a great attitude and friendly disposition
4. software development lifecycle (SDLC) or software development is a plus
5. Project Management Professional certification (PMP) or other PMI
6. Project Management
Collaborate with internal team to develop and maintain project timelines and
budgets according to client contracts.
•       Understand project scope and effectively manage client expectations and
requests
```

Go

Once you have inserted your edited job description document, press the "Go" button as shown above.

You can see the JAVA pop-up below. Make sure you wait for it to show up. It sometimes takes a minute or two. Then hit the "run" button.

Above is the raw result of the word cloud. It is relatively unusable in its current form.

The next step is to reduce the words to five, which should yield three good words. Typically, you can get 20 good keywords out of 30 when using this process. I suggest that you use 20 good keywords in this process. You will see I only will cover one. This is just a repetitive process to get the 20 good keywords.

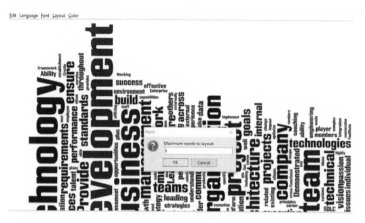

The next step is to make this more usable. Click the "Layout" tab and click on "Horizontal."

Click on the "Layout" tab, then click "Maximum words," enter the number "5" as seen above and click "OK."

team technology business project development

Above you can see the top five keywords from the word cloud. There are two non-keywords: "company" and "business." There is one keyword that may be iffy, which is "team."

team business development leadership project organization technology management company architecture

Above, you can see the top ten keywords from the word cloud. There are three non-keywords: "company," "experience," and "business." There are three keywords that may be iffy, which are: "team," "leadership," and "project."

Above you can see the top 25 keywords from the word cloud. There are nine non-keywords: "company," "ensure," "provide," "organization," "people," "work," "success," "experience," and "business." There are three keywords that may be iffy, which are: "team," "leadership," and "project."

Above is an example of taking one of the keywords we identified in our word cloud: "technology." If we put "technology" in the search box of our word processing program, in this instance Microsoft Word, you will see the occurrences of "technology" in your edited job description document.

As you walk through the document, you can see the modifiers of "technology." These can be used as part of the keyword pairs or keyword strings you can use in your LinkedIn profile.

Passion for *Technology*
Technology **Execution**
Technology **Direction**

Infrastructure *Technology*
Technology **Arena**
Technology **Requirements**
Technology **Architecture**
Technology **Leader**
Technology **Organization**
Technology **Strategy**

Deep Understanding of *Technology*

Technology **Know-How**
Technology **Experience**
Technology **Community**
Technology **Groups**
Technology **Decisions**

The next step is to utilize these keyword pairs and keyword strings and put them into a spreadsheet. Evaluate "The Keyword Pairs Groupings" (rank 0–5).

Now put all your keyword pairs and keyword strings in the spreadsheet. You then evaluate the value of the keywords. You are allowed ten five-ranking keywords pairs or keywords strings which are the most important to you.

You then get rid of the looser keywords by ranking them zero. Most people do not use the one-rankings because the odds are you are not going to use them. Now you have the fun of choosing the two- to four-rankings. The fours should be relatively easy. The twos and threes seem to be the most painful to rank and generally take the most time.

Make Sure You Are Using Nouns And Verbs

You want to use nouns and verbs for keywords. If you are a marketing person, the keyword strings tend to be longer. The example spreadsheet is for marketing and general manager positions. Using more than five or six keywords in a keyword string is getting long and may need to be adjusted.

Track Where You Put The Keywords In Your Profile

When you place your keywords into your LinkedIn profile, you should track where you put them and your frequency of use. In the spreadsheet example, I never used the keywords more than twice. I do not recommend using a keyword string more than four times.

Test Keyword Placement With LinkedIn Search

After you place keywords in your LinkedIn profile, you should test keyword pairs by using LinkedIn search. Warning, a few keywords will search badly as stand-alone keywords. Do not discard them (such as company & organization). There is a process for doing this testing covered in the *More Powerful Search Ranking* book.

The Most Important Keywords:

The most important keywords are your titles.

Your Short Title: CEO, COO, CIO, CMO, CDO

Your Long Title: Chief Executive Officer, Chief Operating Officer, Chief Information Officer, Chief Marketing Officer, Chief Digital Officer

This spreadsheet example is one that I utilized for a client. Please forgive me for obscuring the profile locations, but this is a working example where the LinkedIn profile made page one in search for his position.

	A	B	C	D	E	F
	Key words	Priority	Loc 1	Loc 2	Loc 3	Loc 4
2						
42	Direct experience in Board relations	2	ford			
43	Experience as a spokesperson to strategic partner organizations	2	dec			
44	extensive experience with P&L management	5	ford			
45	Experience in participating at the senior level in mergers & acquisitions	0				
46	private equity experience	3	heart	ford		
47	Experience leading a geographically dispersed team	3	dec			
48	Champions and creates the optimal client experience strategy	3	dec			
49	Client Experience Management	4	ford			
50	Product innovation experience	5	ietna			
51	Demonstrated experience in execution excellence	5	heart			
52	Experience leading cross functional teams	4	ford			
53	Solid knowledge of standard research techniques and tools exp	0				
54	Product strategy	2	MY			
55	Familiarity with client experience concepts and optimization	3	Dec			

Chapter 7
Identify High-Value Areas of Your LinkedIn Profile

Donald J. Wittman, LI SEO, Search Visibility
Be Visible on LinkedIn With a Search Optimized Profile |
LinkedIn Consultant | LinkedIn Training | Best Selling Author

There are two areas of interest on the page view above that is the highest search value area on your profile.

First is your name line. There is quite a bit of valuable real estate after your last name in your profile's last name field. Do not put your last name in the LinkedIn first name field. This may cause problems for being found by name or translating your name fields. This is especially true when you submit your profile for a LinkedIn job opportunity. A name field is defined as all letters, not letters and numbers. If you put something like your phone number in your last name field, you may blow up your job submission. LinkedIn does not permit you to put anything but your name in the name fields. However, it has become an acceptable practice, and LinkedIn has stopped enforcing it for now.

Second is your main headline field. This field is a 120-character field. The default entry in this field by LinkedIn is your title and company from your current position. I suggest this be a keyword statement covered earlier. Your keywords in your main headline field may not rank unless they are in other headline fields.

A reminder, be very careful about using punctuation in these two fields as well as the other headline fields we cover.

Your Current Position Headline

The top line of your current position is the next highest value field in your LinkedIn profile, as seen below. This is also considered your current position field. So make sure you have it in this field. If a recruiter searches using the current position or title search filter, this field is where it searches. If you have multiple positions with the same company, your LinkedIn profile looks a little different than if you did not. This is shown in the first graphic.

Experience

Wittman Technology, LLC - LinkedIn Speaker - LinkedIn Coach - Training - Consulting - Social Media
8 yrs

Advanced LinkedIn Trainer | LinkedIn Consultant | CEO | LinkedIn Training | Social Media | Speaker
2010 – Present · 8 yrs
Greater New York City Area, LinkedIn Consulting, LinkedIn Search Expert, SEO

I work with time-challenged executives on how to build an energized staff, improve employee retention, and ultimately become more productive and profitable by using the power of LinkedIn.

As CTO, I'm in a unique position to help organizations to effectively use LinkedIn to increase their market advantage. In 2012, I figured out a LinkedIn training methodology that can help just about any executive hiring manager find and hire the right talent, streamline the hiring process, and give back the time that they need to grow their companies. As a result, my clients have built energized teams, exceeded productivity, met revenue goals, and have increased their knowledge a... See more

CEO, Corporate LinkedIn Consulting, Corporate LinkedIn Trainer, LinkedIn Speaker, LinkedIn SEO
Dec 2010 – Present · 7 yrs 9 mos
Greater New York City Area | LinkedIn Training, LinkedIn Consultant, Coach, SEO

LINKEDIN CONSULTING

LinkedIn profile Consulting for Job Seekers:
1. Key Word Strategy & Identification... See more

Wittman Technology, LLC - LinkedIn Speaker - LinkedIn Training - LinkedIn Consulting - Social Media
7 yrs 10 mos

Advanced LinkedIn Trainer | LinkedIn Consultant | CEO | LinkedIn Training | Social Media | Speaker

---

Advanced LinkedIn Trainer | LinkedIn Consultant | CEO | LinkedIn Training | Social Media | Speaker

Wittman Technology, LLC - LinkedIn Speaker - LinkedIn Coach - Training - Consulting - Social Media

2010 – Present · 8 yrs
Greater New York City Area, LinkedIn Consulting, LinkedIn Search Expert, SEO
I work with time-challenged executives on how to build an energized staff, improve employee retention, and ultimately become more productive and profitable by using the power of LinkedIn.

Advanced LinkedIn Trainer | LinkedIn Consultant | CEO | LinkedIn Training | Social Media | Speaker

Wittman Technology Speaker , LLC - LinkedIn Training - LinkedIn Consulting - Social Media

Nov 2010 – Present · 8 yrs
Greater New York City Area, LinkedIn Consulting, LinkedIn Search Expert, SEO

Advaced LinkedIn Trainer | LinkedIn Consultant | LinkedIn Training | Social Media |
LinkedIn Speaker

Wittman Technology, LLC - LinkedIn Speaker - LinkedIn Training - LinkedIn Consulting - Social Media

Nov 2010 – Present · 8 yrs
Greater New York City Area, LinkedIn Consulting, LinkedIn Search Expert, SEO

Next LinkedIn Positions

One, two, three positions back are the next highest value fields. They should contain the name of the position you held and potentially equivalent position name. If you have room, you may want to put in the position you are striving to land

If your LINKEDIN PROFILE was on PAGE 1 for your JOB SEARCH or BUSINESS, what kind of success would that bring to the table? LinkedIn is the best place for business people to find other business people.

As a previous CTO, I combine in-depth technology expertise toward the use of LinkedIn. I have a set of processes to get my clients found. For those DIY'ers, I offer a variety of Training Classes and Webinars to help you understand my proven process.

HIGH CHALLENGE JOB SEARCH

The most common complaint, after professionals complete their LinkedIn Profiles, is Head Hunters are not finding them on LinkedIn.

I help Professionals find the right "KEYWORDS" for the position they aspire to and place these words in my client's profile for the best search results.

This is only one of five metrics that are important to LinkedIn Search. This process results in significantly higher profile views and inbound contact rate.

JOB SEARCH PRODUCTIVITY

Another common complaint is they have a Highly Key Worded LinkedIn Profile and my profile views are still low, what do I do now?

Only about 1/3rd of the Head Hunters on LinkedIn have a HR Subscription which allows them to see all LinkedIn members. If LinkedIn Members can't see the other 2/3rd Head Hunters, they can't see you! Optimizing your LinkedIn Profile includes LinkedIn visibility, which drives Head Hunters or Business People to you!

CONTACT ME

I'd welcome the opportunity to schedule a time to talk about your LinkedIn challenges and explore how we may be able to work together. I teach seminars, workshops and provide one-on-one tutoring and coaching to clients looking to strengthen their presence on LinkedIn.

I can be reached at:
email - don@donaldjwittman.com
Telephone - 203-917-4253

Summary

The summary is the second from the bottom of LinkedIn value areas of your profile. It is just above plain text. The real importance of your summary is that it is the first field most recruiters or customers will see. So make the most of it.

Skills & Endorsements

The top three to five skills help LinkedIn build the theme of your profile. It means that if you have CFO skills in the first five skills, it will help you in searching for a CFO position.

Having less than 25 endorsements for any skill will make those particular skills valueless.

LinkedIn has been playing with the search value of skills. At this time, they range from nothing when you have less than 25 endorsements to up to three points, but this ranking value is inconsistent.

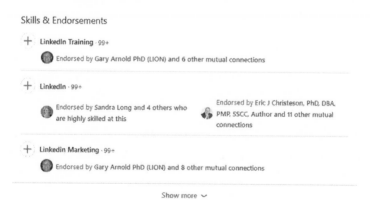

Chapter 8
Conclusion

You now have a lot of work to do to get your LinkedIn profile in good shape. It generally takes a good week of effort to get these tips implemented. The keywording of your profile can be a bit of a problem if you are in a challenging area, such a New York City, Boston, Chicago, Los Angeles, and San Francisco. In these areas, it may take several rounds of changes to rank for the position you really want.

If you need additional help, you can buy my book coming out soon on; *The Job Seekers Guide to Getting Hired on LinkedIn*.

There are two situations where optimizing your profile may not be helpful.

First, if a position you are looking for is highly sought after and there are more people looking for that position, then there are positions available.

Second, there are just none of these positions available in your area. Not having a position you are looking for in your area is becoming more common than not. Do not make your search too narrow initially, or you may be throwing away opportunities.

I wish you all the best in your job search endeavors.

About the Author

Donald J. Wittman is currently Principal at Wittman Technology where he leads high-level consulting projects for technology organizations.

A strong leader and exceptional contributor throughout his career, Mr. Donald J. Wittman has an exceptionally broad base of experience in information technology, systems security, data center operations, systems engineering, IT governance, and business continuance.

From his early days on the IT management fast-track at MCI Telecom, Philip Morris, Priceline Group, to his more recent assignment as Vice President & Chief Technology Officer at Adaptive Marketing/Vertrue, an Internet services provider, Mr. Wittman has distinguished himself with a long list of high-impact contributions: IT innovation, turnaround/revitalizations, efficiency gains, large-scale project management, network migrations and advances in system security—transforming IT from a cost center into a full-fledged business partner that creates value and delivers revenue and profits.

Skilled at finding practical solutions to complex technical and operational financial issues, Mr. Wittman is regarded as a "full spectrum leader"—one who shapes the future, delivers results, energizes the team, builds strong relationships and models personal integrity and accountability. His intellect and considerable management talents are evident in his history of taking multi-million-dollar systems and software development projects from the drawing board all the way through to a smooth and successful implementation.

Mr. Wittman has shown himself to be a polished communicator, effective consensus-builder, and a strong negotiator. He has managed dozens of major IT initiatives and has successfully negotiated on major capital equipment purchases, bundled software services, and data center commitments, among others. In addition, he has enjoyed outstanding success as a strategic planner and architect of change, consistently delivering improved project performance, higher levels of efficiency, and better ROIs.

Mr. Wittman's skills and talents can be summarized in just a few short words; enterprise, vision, technical excellence, and sound business judgment.

Mr. Wittman's non-business interests range from being a DIY handyman since a teenager to college and amateur theater in his earlier years to snowmobiling, traveling, and building big engines for American heavy-metal cars—especially his 1960 Corvette.

Made in the USA
Middletown, DE
27 July 2019